What Is a Sacrament?

Most Catholics recognize that sacraments are an important part of life in the church. They see them as significant moments that mark transitions in life. They bring their babies to be baptized and send their second graders to prepare for First Communion. They come to the church to be married and ask for the anointing when someone is seriously ill.

Sacraments, however, are much more than mileposts in the spiritual life. The Second Vatican Council (1962–65) called for a renewal of the liturgy that included revising all the sacraments. The purpose of the revision was to re-think our understanding of these basic actions that shape our identity in the church. In their first document, the Constitution on the Sacred Liturgy, issued in 1963, the council fathers spoke of the importance of the sacraments for the Christian life:

> The purpose of the sacraments is to sanctify people, to build up the body of Christ, and, finally, to worship God. Because they are signs they also belong in the realm of instruction. They not only presuppose faith, but by words and objects they also nourish, strengthen, and express it. That is why they are called sacraments of faith. They do, indeed, confer grace, but, in addition, the very act of celebrating them is most effective in making people ready to receive this grace to their profit, to worship God duly, and to practice charity.
>
> It is, therefore, of the greatest importance that the faithful should easily understand the symbolism of the sacraments and eagerly frequent those sacraments which were instituted to nourish the Christian life (no. 59).

Helping people to readily understand the sacramental signs is the goal of this series of booklets.

Though this booklet focuses on the sacrament of confirmation, there are basic principles that can help us to understand all the sacraments, for they share some fundamental characteristics.

SACRAMENTS ARE HUMAN ACTIVITIES

In confirmation, anointing with the scented oil, called chrism, symbolizes the presence of the Holy Spirit.

First, the sacraments are human activities. We often think of the sacraments in terms of the elements of creation that we use: water, oil, bread and wine, etc. Yet the sacraments are better understood as the actions that we do with those elements, and those actions are all basic human gestures. We wash bodies, anoint foreheads, eat bread and drink wine, touch and caress the sick, lay on hands as a gesture of conferring power, etc. These human actions become the means of encountering the Lord.

These actions have become rituals; we follow familiar patterns of movement and gesture and recite the official words of the rite. We perform these rituals as our ancestors did. Nonetheless, rituals are revised and updated from time to time to keep them fresh and true to their original purpose.

Our ritual actions are symbolic, giving us a real and concrete way to experience or express something that is otherwise abstract. A symbol contains the reality it expresses. A kiss, for example, somehow contains the love it expresses, though it does not exhaust that love. So, too, the Eucharistic meal contains the presence of Jesus, though it does not exhaust that presence.

Scripture clarifies the symbols we use. "I will give you a new heart and place a new Spirit within you" (Ezek 36:26).

All the sacraments also rely on the word of God. The prayers and formulas of the rituals have been drawn from the Bible, and the celebrations always include a formal proclamation of the word of God. The word clarifies the meaning of the symbols we use. Proclaiming God's word in the celebration also reminds us that our actions are always a response to what God has done for us.

SACRAMENTS ARE ACTIONS OF THE CHURCH COMMUNITY

The ritual actions that we carry out in the sacraments are always communal actions. This may be the most important realization in our renewed understanding of the sacraments. They are the actions of the church community, not just of the presider or the recipient. As the Constitution on the

UNDERSTANDING

THE

SACRAMENTS

Confirmation

Lawrence E. Mick

Published by Liturgical Press, Collegeville, Minnesota.
www.litpress.org

Design by David Manahan, O.S.B.
Photos: cover, pages 5, 11, The Crosiers; pages 7, 13, 15, 18, W. P.
Wittman.

ISBN 978-0-8146-3189-8

Sacred Liturgy puts it: "It is very much the wish of the church that all the faithful should be led to take that full, conscious, and active part in liturgical celebrations which is demanded by the very nature of the liturgy" (no. 14). Liturgy is the public worship of the church in its various forms. Though we may celebrate around an individual or a group of people receiving a sacrament, we all celebrate the sacrament together. A sacrament is the action of the church, and its meaning and effects are not limited to those around whom we celebrate.

"Liturgy" comes from the Greek meaning "work of the people" and refers to the various forms of public worship of the church.

One primary effect of any sacrament is to form us for mission. Each sacrament, in its own way, strengthens us to carry on the mission of Christ in the world today. Sacraments, then, are necessary to the life of the community and the furtherance of its mission. They make the church what Christ intends it to be, and they make each of us what Christ intends us to become.

SACRAMENTS ARE THE ACTION OF CHRIST

At the same time, because the church is the Body of Christ, the action of a sacrament is also the action of Christ. The Constitution on the Sacred Liturgy puts it this way: "By his power he is present in the sacraments, so that when anybody baptizes it is really Christ himself who baptizes" (no. 7).

The church has long taught that the power of a sacrament is not dependent on the ability or holiness of the priest, bishop, or deacon presiding. The sacrament is effective even if the minister is unworthy or sinful. It does not ultimately depend on the minister, for it is Christ who acts through the gathered community, which is his Body.

The encounter with Christ in the sacraments is possible only through faith. That's why baptism is the first sacrament and the precondition for all the others. It is the sacrament of initial faith, which is a response to God's grace calling a person to belief. The sacraments express our faith and also nourish and strengthen faith, because they bring us into contact with the living Christ.

The tradition speaks of sacraments giving grace. That is ultimately a way of saying that they bring us into contact with Christ and enable us to deepen our friendship with the Lord. Grace is, at root, that relationship, and the encounter with Christ in a sacrament deepens that friendship.

Sacraments are a part of our relationship with God, a part of our faith life. They express what God is already doing in our lives and move us further along the road of conversion and spiritual growth. Sacraments should never be viewed as isolated moments in our lives. They depend on a process that leads up to the moment of celebration and flows from that moment into our future. Sacraments require preparation on the part of the individual and on the part of the community. Sacraments affect the life of the individual and the community far beyond the celebration itself.

Confirmation
Celebrating the Spirit of God

As I was working on this booklet, I heard on the radio a quote from a Western diplomat talking about elections in Lebanon. He said: "If you think you understand Lebanese politics, it obviously hasn't been explained to you properly." Many people feel that something similar could be said about the sacrament of confirmation. Explaining it properly is no simple task, and the explanation may still leave us less than certain of this sacrament's meaning.

Many people experience confusion about this sacrament at the parish level. The age for confirmation varies from diocese to diocese and from one parish to the next. Even in the same parish, some young children are confirmed when they are baptized at the Easter Vigil, while children baptized as infants are required to wait for confirmation until they are older. Picking up different books and listening to different speakers talk about confirmation makes one wonder if they are all discussing the same sacrament.

One short statement from the Second Vatican Council's Constitution on the Sacred Liturgy (1963), however, provides us the key to understanding confirmation: "The rite of confirmation is to be revised also so that the intimate connection of this sacrament with the whole of Christian initiation may be shown more clearly" (no. 71). In other words, confirmation does not stand alone. Whether or not they are celebrated at the same time, confirmation, baptism, and Eucharist are intimately connected. This sacrament is called "confirmation" because it confirms or reaffirms the significance of baptism (whether that was celebrated a few minutes or several years earlier) and the gift of the Holy Spirit received in baptism.

A Look at History

This sacrament has had a difficult life. Through the centuries people in the church have used it to serve many different needs. These uses are so different from one another that it is easy to understand why the meaning of this sacrament is a puzzle for many people today.

Paul Turner, in his excellent study entitled *Confirmation: The Baby in Solomon's Court* (Paulist Press, 1993), has described no fewer than seven different rituals in use in various churches today, all called confirmation. He sees these seven as deriving ultimately from three different models in early Christianity: the completion of the rite of baptism, the reconciliation of heretics, and the post-baptismal anointing postponed until some time after baptism. All three of these models are in use in the church today. Adults and children old enough for instruction are confirmed when they are baptized. Those baptized as infants are confirmed years later. And those who join the Catholic Church who were baptized in another denomination are received with a rite that includes confirmation (these people aren't called heretics today, but that was the term used in early Christianity).

A look at church history reveals the context for these three ancient roots of confirmation. Evidence

from the early days of the church is very limited. We naturally look to the New Testament to see how the first Christians celebrated the gift of the Holy Spirit. However, despite various hints about the role of the Holy Spirit in the lives of Christians, the New Testament gives us no real evidence for any rite that we would recognize as confirmation. For several centuries after the New Testament period, Christians would have been very puzzled if we had asked them about the sacrament of confirmation. What we have come to know as a separate sacrament was for them simply a part of the rite of baptism, the celebration of initiation by which a person became a Christian.

ANCIENT INITIATION RITUALS

The celebration of initiation varied from place to place and from time to time, so it would take a large book to describe it in detail in all its variations in these centuries. Instead, we will examine here a typical outline of elements that can give us a sense of the experience. Such a rite, normally celebrated at the Easter Vigil for candidates who had long prepared for initiation, would begin with the candidates leaving the assembly to go to the baptistery, often a separate building near the entrance to the church. Once there, they would renounce Satan, perhaps facing the west and spitting at him; then facing the east, they would commit themselves to Christ. After this they would strip completely, leaving their old life (and old clothes) behind. They would be anointed with oil over their whole bodies, preparing for the crucial contest with the power of evil like athletes being rubbed down before a match. After the blessing of the font, which would be big enough for the person to be immersed, the candidates would enter the water, perhaps going down three steps into a pool. There they were immersed three times in the name of the Father and of the Son and of the Holy Spirit. Coming out of the water, they would be clothed in white garments.

At this point the candidates would return to the full assembly, where the bishop was waiting with the faithful. Greeted with acclamations, they would then be anointed by the bishop with the oil called chrism and greeted with the kiss of peace. Now members of the faithful, they would join the full assembly for the celebration of the Easter Eucharist, sharing in Communion for the first time. The anointing by the bishop after the baptismal bath is the ancient root of what we know as confirmation.

As this description of initiation suggests, this anointing was a brief part of a much larger rite. It was unique, however, in that it was done by the bishop, while the earlier parts of the rite were the responsibility of the presbyter (priest) or deacon (or deaconess). It is the required presence of the bishop that led to confirmation becoming a separate sacrament in the West.

SEPARATION FROM BAPTISM

As long as dioceses were small and the bishop always presided at Easter initiations, there was no problem. But when that was no longer possible due to the increasing size of the church, the question arose about what to do with that portion of initiation when the bishop was not present. In the East the decision was made that whoever presided at the Easter rites would do the anointing. Thus among Eastern churches, the anointing or chrismation is, to this day, celebrated immediately after the water bath of baptism, whether the initiate is an adult or an infant.

In the West, however, Pope Innocent I insisted in the year 412 that this anointing had to be done by the bishop, so it was delayed until he was available. Thus it became separated from the baptismal ritual. This is the first time we find the ritual being called confirmation, as the bishop was confirming the baptism at which a priest had presided.

At first confirmation was still celebrated shortly after the Easter Vigil, during Easter week or at least in the Easter season, but gradually it began to be pushed back further and further. Through the centuries we can see the normal age for this completion of initiation getting older and older, until it was generally celebrated at age fourteen.

As this happened, First Communion was often also delayed, since it was properly received only after confirmation. At the beginning of the twentieth century, Pope Pius X lowered the age for First Communion to seven to encourage more frequent Communion, and confirmation was left hanging, as it were, in midair, now fully removed from the initiation celebration in most people's minds.

So the first of Turner's historical models was an anointing that was clearly part of baptism. Moving that anointing until later, eventually many years after baptism, is seen as a separate model because it lost its roots in initiation and came to be seen as a sacrament of Christian maturity.

The third historical source of confirmation is the reconciliation of heretics and schismatics. Even before confirmation was separated from baptism, the church was using similar rituals to readmit those who had broken their union with the church (schismatics) and those who had been baptized by heretics (those who rejected some part of Catholic belief). Heretics or those baptized by them were generally reconciled with an anointing, while schismatics were commonly reconciled with the laying on of hands. Even though we don't call them heretics today, this model is reflected in the contemporary practice of confirming those who join the Catholic Church after having been baptized in another Christian denomination. Their baptism is recognized as valid baptism, but they still require an initiation rite to become Catholic.

Those baptized into other Christian churches are welcomed into the Catholic Church with the Rite of Reception, usually including confirmation and First Communion.

Multiple Patterns in Place

Turner suggests that the church needs to decide just where confirmation belongs. As we noted at the beginning of this booklet, the Second Vatican Council called the church to recover the baptismal character of this sacrament. Yet the revised rites continue to support several understandings of confirmation. The Rite of Christian Initiation of Adults (RCIA), issued in 1972, takes a strong stand for unifying baptism and confirmation: ". . . adults are not to be baptized without receiving confirmation immediately afterward, unless some serious reason stands in the way. The conjunction of the two celebrations signifies the unity of the paschal mystery, the close link between the mission of the Son and the outpouring of the Holy Spirit, and the connection between the two sacraments through which the Son and the Holy Spirit come from the Father to those who are baptized" (no. 215). To make these confirmations possible, the rite authorizes the presider at the initiation of adults to confirm them, whether that is a bishop or a priest.

It is important to note that this principle applies not just to adults but also to children old enough to receive instruction. Such children go through a process of preparation similar to the adult process, and they are baptized, confirmed, and given First Eucharist at the Easter Vigil along with the adult initiates. This rule is not optional but required by canon law; it is not permitted to delay the confirmation of such children until the "usual age" for confirmation of those baptized in infancy. Since they are old enough for formation, they are to receive all three sacraments of initiation in the same celebration.

The celebration of the sacraments of initiation has not been unified for children baptized as infants. This means that most parishes have two patterns of confirmation for children: immediately after baptism for child catechumens and separated from baptism by many years for children baptized as infants. And the Rite of Christian Initiation of Adults provides for reception of people baptized in other churches with a rite that includes confirmation. So all three of the ancient models are being used in the contemporary church.

Initiation and Conversion

Nevertheless, we should always remember that this sacrament is closely linked to baptism. The revised Rite of Confirmation issued in 1971 reflects this linkage in several ways. The candidates for confirmation renew their baptismal vows during the celebration. They are encouraged to have their baptismal godparents as sponsors for this sacrament as well, and they are also encouraged to use their baptismal names as confirmation names (although another sponsor or name may be chosen). The sacrament is now regularly celebrated within the Eucharist, thus reminding us of the ancient practice of celebrating baptism, confirmation, and Eucharist as one initiatory rite.

Because confirmation is a sacrament of initiation, it is about conversion. Conversion is an ongoing process of conforming to the Christian way of life. We all are called to a life of continual conversion, gradually rooting out sin and selfishness and giving our lives more and more completely to Christ. Nevertheless, one's

The link to baptism is expressed by the renewal of baptism vows.

11

initial conversion is the basis for the celebration of the initiation sacraments. These sacraments celebrate the conversion that God is bringing about in the lives of the candidates. When they are celebrated with adults in the RCIA, they celebrate a conversion that has already reached a certain degree of maturity through the catechumenate formation process. When initiation begins in infancy, the sacramental celebration anticipates the conversion and presumes that this conversion will be fostered in the months and years ahead. If there is no reasonable assurance that this will happen, then the celebration of baptism must be delayed until it can be assured.

As with all the sacraments, in confirmation the Christian community celebrates what God has been doing in the lives of those to be confirmed. If the sacrament is celebrated with an infant, as it is in the Eastern Church and among many Hispanics, then it celebrates the call of God mediated through the child's parents, just as baptism celebrates that call. If confirmation is celebrated with older children or adults, then the community celebrates the presence and action of the Holy Spirit in the candidates, who received that Spirit in baptism.

Whenever the sacrament is celebrated, the same principle applies. God expects a response that is appropriate for the age of the candidate. With an infant, that response comes through the parents of the child; with an older candidate, some response should be evident in the life of the person being confirmed. The nature of that response, of course, will depend on the age and personality of the candidate, so we don't look for a truly adult response from a seven-year-old or a twelve-year-old who is confirmed.

Confirmation has always been focused on the gift of the Holy Spirit, seen often as the continuation of the Pentecost event. Yet the church has also always associated the gift of the Spirit with baptism. Anyone who has taught about this sacrament knows the questions this raises: Do we get another dose of the Spirit? Wasn't the Spirit's coming at baptism effective? Why do we need confirmation at all? As long as the anointing was part of the same ceremony with baptism, there was no problem. In that framework, the anointing and laying on of hands were the focus for the community's celebration of the gift of the Spirit, while the water bath was the focus of incorporation into the death and resurrection of Christ. Once they were separated, however, the problems were inevitable.

The same issue arises with other aspects of the meaning of confirmation. Is it the sacrament of Christian witness? Yes, because the Spirit is the power within us that enables us to witness. But doesn't baptism already commit us and empower us to witness? Does confirmation make us soldiers of Christ, able to suffer for him if necessary? Yes, the Spirit gives courage to profess our faith even under persecution. But isn't this also true of baptism?

One approach that has been popular for centuries is to see baptism as the sacrament of Christian infancy and confirmation as the sacrament of Christian maturity. The main difficulty with this approach is the definition of "Christian maturity." Many people have incorrectly identified Christian maturity with either the beginning or the end of puberty. On this principle many parishes have pushed the age of confirmation back further and further in quest of some magic age when the candidates will be "mature." "Christian maturity" refers rather to maturity in faith. But maturity is a relative term. A ten-year-old is acting maturely when he acts like a ten-year-old. The church's tradition of celebrating initiation in its fullness with both adults and children points out the inadequacy of this approach. If baptism can be celebrated with infants, so can confirmation. It is the completion of baptism, but it is not the sacrament of Christian adolescence.

When the initiation sacraments are celebrated in one unified liturgy, as at the Easter Vigil, then the function of confirmation is to focus our attention on the gift of the Spirit that comes to us in baptism. The water bath focuses our attention on dying and rising with Christ, sharing in his paschal mystery. The anointing follows immediately, and there is little question of when the Spirit is given. Our tradition is clear that the Holy Spirit comes with baptism. When the two sacraments are celebrated together, the difference is the emphasis or focus of each. When they are celebrated years apart, the difference is still the same.

The Holy Spirit seeks to draw us further into the divine life of the Trinity and further into the life of the Body of Christ, the church.

What the community celebrates in this sacrament, regardless of the age of the candidates, is the presence and action of the Holy Spirit. This is the Spirit that animates and unites the Christian community of faith. This is the Spirit that dwells in each of us from the day we are baptized. This is the Spirit who is given to us as God's most precious gift. This is the Spirit who is to be our strength and our guide in living the Christian life.

We often speak of receiving the Holy Spirit in confirmation, but if that Spirit has been given in baptism, this language can be confusing. When confirmation is celebrated immediately after baptism, we recognize the giving of the Holy Spirit in that full initiation liturgy. When it is celebrated years after baptism, the real issue is whether that gift, already given in baptism, has been fully received so that it bears fruit in the life of the candidate. Those who were baptized as infants often need to become more aware of the gift they have received. They need to learn to listen to the Holy Spirit and follow the Spirit's guidance. The preparation for and celebration of confirmation can be the occasion for growing into life in the Spirit in a more conscious and complete way. The function of confirmation is to focus our attention on the gift of the Spirit, whether the sacrament is celebrated at the same time as baptism or years later.

The Candidates and the Community

If the sacrament of confirmation is to be celebrated with integrity and honesty, then the community must see some signs of conversion in the candidates. There is often a problem when students are prepared for confirmation as a class, with the assumption that all will celebrate the sacrament at the same time. This can prevent any real discernment of conversion or the action of the Spirit in the lives of the candidates. It can help if parish leaders make clear the importance of discernment and encourage candidates, parents, sponsors, and catechists to be aware of the need for at least some signs of ongoing conversion. If none can

14

be discerned in the life of a particular candidate, the celebration of the sacrament with that candidate should be postponed.

A better solution, perhaps, is to take the sacrament out of the "class" mentality. In the RCIA, it is clear that each person is to be treated individually, respecting his or her own rate of growth and accepting that God's timing may be different from ours. While some parishes deal with catechumens as a "class," expecting all to be initiated at the same time, that is clearly not the intent of the rite. This might make us question the common assumption that confirmation and First Eucharist should be celebrated as classes rather than discerning the conversion process as it occurs in each candidate.

This attention to the readiness of the candidates is important for a true celebration, yet more is needed. If the sacraments are celebrations of the whole church, then the whole church must be involved with the candidates in their conversion process. As the RCIA has helped us to understand, the initiation of new members into the church "is the responsibility of all the baptized" (no. 9). All the faithful are expected to take responsibility for those being initiated. They support them by prayer and fasting, they join with them in prayer and study, they make them feel welcome and give them, by example, insight into the way of life of the Christian community. This same concern should also surround those who are baptized as infants and those who are confirmed and brought to First Eucharist as children. The community should manifest its interest and support as these candidates go through their gradual conversion, learning and growing in the life of Christ.

At the same time, the community itself benefits from this interaction as well. Every time initiation is celebrated around an individual or a group of individuals, the whole community is drawn once again into the conversion process. The witness of those being initiated is a powerful example to the rest of the church. The candidates are living reminders of the community's own initiation and the commitment that it entails. While the community supports those receiving the sacrament, it is also challenged by them to live up to its own identity as a people always in the process of deepening its own level of conversion. It may well be that lack of regular experience of the initiation sacraments by most Catholics is a major cause of the spiritual apathy in so many parishes. These celebrations can serve as a potent reminder of who we are as a people and of what life in Christ really means.

Confirmation challenges the community to deepen its level of conversion.

Whenever the community celebrates a dimension of its life and conversion, that dimension is strengthened and deepened. In confirmation the whole community should become more aware of the Spirit, more open to divine guidance, and more aware of the gifts they have received. Those around whom the community celebrates would naturally experience these effects even more deeply than the rest of the community, though of course this is not automatic. Like all spiritual effects of the sacraments, these depend on our preparation and our openness to the action of God. This is true for all who celebrate the sacrament, both the recipients and the rest of the community. The way these effects are experienced will also vary depending on the age of the recipients. God takes each of us at our own stage of growth and gives gifts appropriate to our age and needs. But the church is always celebrating the gifts and presence of the Spirit in her midst.

Preparation for the celebration of confirmation, then, should prompt the whole parish community to reflect on the role of the Holy Spirit, not only in individual lives but in the life of the community as well. If we are initiating people into a community that lives by the Spirit, the presence and action of the Spirit should be evident in the community. The sacraments initiate people into a communal life. If that life is not marked by the guidance of the Spirit, the celebration of confirmation will ring hollow.

LOOKING TO THE FUTURE

The history of the sacrament of confirmation suggests various options for its celebration in the years ahead. All three sacraments of initiation (baptism, confirmation, Eucharist) can be celebrated in one ceremony in the ancient pattern. This is the official pattern for adults and children who join the church through the catechumenate. Some have suggested that we ought to celebrate all three sacraments with infants, too, as was done in the early church and is still done in the tradition of the East. Though this option is not possible within current church law, the future may see more openness to such adaptation.

Some parishes and dioceses have restored the traditional order: baptism, confirmation, and then Eucharist. In this pattern, confirmation is normally celebrated during the same Mass as First Communion. In most parishes, however, the twentieth-century pattern of baptism, Eucharist, and then confirmation seems likely to remain common for the foreseeable future.

Whatever pattern is followed in a given parish and at whatever age a person is confirmed, several basic insights drawn from the history and theology of the sacrament should always be kept in mind.

Confirmation Is Linked to Baptism

The first, of course, is the baptismal connection. Those preparing for confirmation should reflect on the significance of their baptism and challenge themselves to live up to its meaning. Those who guide candidates should encourage them to deepen their appreciation of their baptismal name. If it is the name of a saint, getting to know more about that saint may be helpful. Reflection on and discussion of the baptismal promises, which will be renewed in the confirmation ritual, can also be helpful. It is important to remember that we renew these promises each Easter. Confirmation is not the only time that we renew our baptismal commitment.

If one of the baptismal godparents can adequately fulfill the role of confirmation sponsor, that option should be encouraged as well. It is more important, of course, to have a sponsor who can serve as a model of faithful living and support for the one being confirmed. The sponsor serves as the candidate's partner in the whole experience, offering support through presence and prayer, sharing faith, and calling the candidate to a deeper commitment by example. Experience with catechumens suggests that the sponsor is one of the most important dimensions of the initiation experience. If a baptismal godparent can fill the role well, then that is the preferred choice. If neither godparent can do so, then another sponsor should be chosen. Note that the sponsor does not have to be of the same gender as the

candidate. A sponsor must be a Catholic who has received all three sacraments of initiation and is leading a life "in harmony with the faith" (Canon 874). Normally a sponsor must be at least sixteen years of age. The Rite of Confirmation says that even "the parents themselves may present their children for confirmation" (no. 5). This seems to conflict with canon law, which prohibits parents as sponsors; the Commission on the Code of Canon Law resolved the conflict by noting that sponsors are not strictly required for confirmation (Canon 892), so parents would not really be sponsors in such a case. That is really a technical sort of solution, however; the role of the sponsor is important and parents presumably are already involved in their child's formation, so having another sponsor is certainly recommended.

Confirmation Is about Conversion

The second insight is that confirmation, as an initiation sacrament, is about conversion. If the sacrament has any beneficial effects, they will foster the deeper conversion of the person confirmed. Preparation for the sacrament should prompt self-examination about the depth of one's commitment to Christ and how fully one has learned to live in the Holy Spirit. The work of the Spirit is especially the work of conversion, for the Spirit dwells within us, nearer to us than we are to ourselves, and seeks always to draw us further into the divine life of the Trinity.

Conversion has many dimensions, for it involves a personal relationship with the Lord, a change of life based on gospel principles, a relationship to all those who form the Body of Christ, and a commitment of self-sacrificing love and service to others in the name of Christ. Initiation into the Christian community involves all these aspects, for it is incorporation into a community united by the same Lord, living the gospel way of life, and seeking to love all people as God loves them. Confirmation, as a powerful experience of the Spirit, should lead to a fuller and deeper incorporation into this community and its life.